PEOP

CH00642841

THE HUMAN STORIES BEHIND SOUTH WALES' INDUSTRIAL HERITAGE

© HERIAN 2009

First published by HERIAN in 2009
All rights reserved

Designed by www.dispirito.co.uk

ISBN: 978–0–9563027–0–0

ETIFEDDIAETH AR WAITH
HERIAN
HERITAGE IN ACTION

◄ Collecting coal at Cwmcynon Tip during the 1984-85 Miner's Strike.

PEOPLE POWER

This is a book about the people who powered the Industrial Revolution in south Wales: the colliers and quarrymen who cut and hauled raw materials for industry; the nameless and forgotten men, women and children who laboured in ironworks and factories; the pioneering engineers and inventors, whose ideas and designs made the Industrial Revolution happen; and the wealthy entrepreneurs and old money families who financed new industrial processes and innovative transport schemes.

Here we attempt to tell the people's story. There's not enough space to tell everyone's story but we've chosen some of our favourites. We also look at the 'people power' which expressed itself through movements such as the Scotch Cattle, the Rebecca Riots and Chartism, as men and women from south Wales fought to secure the freedoms and political rights we take for granted today, paving the way for modern democracy around the world.

WITH THANKS TO

HERIAN – Jeff Pride, Enid Voss, Ruth Taylor Davies and Kim Colebrook – for their support and encouragement. Special thanks to Les James, University of Newport, for his guidance and Maria Dispirito for her creativity in designing People Power.

I would like to thank the National Library of Wales and Nick Kelland of Rhondda Cynon Taff Libraries' Digital Archive for permission to reproduce images. Thanks also to the following for their help in locating images and allowing their reproduction here: Katrina Coopey in the Local Studies Department, Cardiff Libraries and Information Service, Susan Edwards at the Glamorgan Record Office, Claire Hamer at Cardiff City Council, Andrew Helme at The Nelson Museum and Local History Centre in Monmouth, Rachel Lovering at Newport Museum and Art Gallery, Richard Porch at Swansea City Council and Scott Reid at Cyfarthfa Castle Museum and Art Gallery.

◄ River Level Colliery before 1916.

CONTENTS

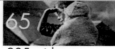

PEOPLE POWER

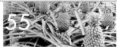

Setting the scene

Imagine a rural landscape dotted with farmhouses and cottages, where just a few people live farming the land, and industry focuses on woollen and textile production. Across this landscape seams of ironstone and coal outcrop close to the surface and swiftly flowing rivers provide power – all the mineral wealth and natural resources needed to start an industrial revolution. Over time charcoal-fired iron production spreads across these valleys and by the eighteenth century three places on the edge of the south Wales coalfield have become centres of innovative metal technology – the Wye Valley making wire, Pontypool producing tinplate and Neath making copper.

Fast forward 50 years. Something has happened along a narrow stretch of the Heads of the Valleys between Blaenavon and Hirwaun. This landscape is now dotted with mines and quarries extracting ironstone, coal and limestone, the raw materials for new coke-fired ironworks which spring up between 1780 and 1830, making possible the mass production of iron. Never before have so many people moved so rapidly into one small part of Wales. The greatest concentration of ironworks develops in Merthyr Tydfil and by 1830 it's become the largest town in Wales and the iron capital of the world. For the first time in history the census records show that more people are employed in industry than in agriculture. Wales has become the first Industrial Nation.

During the first half of the nineteenth century only the coal measures of the 'Black Domain', between Nelson and Crumlin in Monmouthshire, are exploited by the sale coal industry. Coal is transported along the newly opened Monmouthshire Canal to be sold in the Bristol Channel ports. For a while the surrounding Valleys remain unscathed; deep mines require costly investment in pumping and winding technology.

In the iron producing areas the manufacture of steel takes over in the 1850s. By the end of the century metal production in the Valleys is in decline. Steel making moves to coastal locations at Llanwern, Port Talbot and Llanelli, with the exception of Dowlais and Ebbw Vale.

South Wales' coal 'Klondyke' doesn't start until 1870. Its impact is greater than anything seen before. The scale of inward migration matches that into the USA. Row upon row of terraced houses are built for the thousands of migrants who move here to work in the coal mines. Around the world 'Rhondda' becomes synonymous with coal.

Industry changes the landscape and changes lives. Terraces and workingmen's halls, chapels and graveyards all tell stories of the collective struggle and personal suffering of many. The Industrial Revolution also brings wealth and power to south Wales, manifested in grand buildings such as Cyfarthfa Castle, Castell Coch and the Coal Exchange, visible reminders today of the remarkable transformation of south Wales.

2

◢ Penry Williams' painting shows the amazing architecture of the Bute Ironworks at Rhymney, around 1830.

3

The move to industry

In 1770 the largest town in Wales was Carmarthen, with a population of four thousand. Across Wales most people worked on the land. Small numbers worked in fishing, quarries, mines, charcoal-fired iron works and woollen enterprises, often combining their work with agriculture. But from the late 1700s new jobs began to lure people into the Valleys of south Wales, where an iron worker could earn three times as much as a farm labourer. Most migrants didn't move far - from Carmarthenshire and Cardiganshire, Brecknockshire and Monmouthshire. Some moved temporarily, working in the coal and iron towns during the winter months and returning to the countryside for the summer harvest.

Later in the nineteenth and twentieth century migrants came in large numbers from further afield and from other countries: Wales was second only to the USA in terms of the rate of immigration, the only country in Europe not to suffer net emigration to America. One hundred and thirty thousand people moved into the Valleys between 1904 and 1914.

People left jobs on the land for jobs, quite literally, in the land – in coal mines and quarries, and working 'entombed' in huge ironworks. As Aneurin Bevan, who started work underground aged fourteen, wrote, *'In other trades, there are a thousand diversions to break the monotony of work – the passing traffic, the morning newspaper, above all the sky, the sunshine, the wind and the rain. The miner has none of these. Everyday for eight hours he dies, gives up a slice of his life and buries himself.'*

◄ David Dan Evans was photographed after his first day at work. He was born in 1899 in Llandyssul, Cardiganshire where his father worked as a farm labourer. By the 1901 census his father had moved to the Rhondda and was working as a coal miner. David joins him there, starting work when he is just thirteen.

5

Trips to study metallurgy in Europe had been part of John Henry Vivian's education. As well as detailing visits to mines in Germany and Poland, his journal describes meeting Napoleon Bonaparte on the island of Elba, shortly before the Battle of Waterloo.

Copperopolis

By 1790 Swansea had overtaken Carmarthen as Wales' largest town. Swansea was the earliest of the south Wales ports to develop and was also Wales' main coal port by 1790 (Cardiff and Newport didn't catch up until the 1860s). In the seventeenth century most copper was made in central Europe, but by 1790 the Swansea area had become the centre of world copper production. Copper put Swansea on the map.

Thomas Williams who created the Parys Mine Company in 1778, which mined copper reserves in Anglesey, was crucial to this development. Williams had a monopoly control of copper ore and invested heavily in the Swansea area. The advantage of moving copper ore near to the source of the coal needed to smelt it had long been recognised. It explains the growth of the copper industry, using ores brought in by sea, along the coast between Port Talbot and Llanelli during the early nineteenth century. Three tons of coal would smelt one ton of copper, so it was cheaper to transport copper ore than coal.

Most people employed in the copper industry worked in the extremely hot and dangerous conditions of the copper smelters. Metallurgy skills learnt on the job were passed from father to son. Women and children were also employed to push barrows of copper ore to be crushed. For many years these men and women produced ninety percent of the world's copper, making everything from copper ingots and copper tubes to naval brass and super phosphate fertilizers. In the early days they made copper bangles called 'popo manilas' which were traded for slaves in West Africa. Later they manufactured the copper which clad the hulls of Britain's warships.

One family came to dominate copper production in Swansea. A Cornish copper mine and copper works owner, John Henry Vivian (1785 – 1855), went into partnership with his sons, Richard Henry Vivian and John Henry Vivian, in 1809 establishing the Hafod Copper Works beside the Swansea Canal and the River Tawe. From their initial investment of £50,000 the Vivian family prospered, despite competition from many previously established companies such as the White Rock Copper Works and the Middle and Upper Bank Works. In 1828 another Cornish firm had set up the Morfa Copper Works beside the Hafod Works. A high stone wall separated the two enterprises and fearing industrial espionage Morfa employees were told not to talk to their neighbours! Spies were even sent from other countries to try and steal the knowledge which had made Swansea the world centre of copper smelting and won it the name of Copperopolis.

By the 1840s the Hafod Works had become one of the largest industrial enterprises in Europe. John Henry Vivian was the driving force behind the business which had a capital value of over £1.2m in the 1880s. The Vivians built a community for their copper workers called Trevivian (now known as Hafod), each house having a ty bach (toilet), coal house, pig sty and garden. There was also a school and church.

A lethal by-product of the copper industry was arsenic. Noxious sulphuric fumes stunted and killed vegetation for miles around, whilst polluted air and water affected the health of workers and the people who lived nearby. Unbelievably, whilst all this industrial activity was happening in the Swansea Valley, the town of Swansea was trying to establish itself as a fashionable resort by the sea. Men and women were working in the stinking copper works whilst 'up wind' affluent visitors bathed on Swansea beach.

After 1807 visitors could travel around Swansea Bay to Mumbles on the world's first passenger railway, a horse drawn carriage which carried twelve people. The Mumbles Railway was built to link Swansea with the quarries and mines at Mumbles and Clyne, but it became a popular people mover. Previously the only way to reach Mumbles had been to walk along the beach.

Kitty was painted by an English artist George Delamotte, who visited Swansea in the 1810s and 1820s. Behind Kitty you can see people bathing in Swansea Bay.

 Francis Crawshay (1811 – 1878).

 The Tin Works at Trefforest around 1840, about the time Francis Crawshay commissioned a set of portraits of his workers from a well known Victorian artist, W. J. Chapman.

Working iron and steel

By the eighteenth century charcoal-fired iron industries were found right across the Valleys. Three centres of innovative metal making had developed on the edge of the coalfield – at Pontypool, around Neath and Swansea and in the Wye Valley. Then, between 1780 and 1830 new ironworks developed along the Heads of the Valleys, using state-of-the-art technology imported from Shropshire, which enabled the construction of mass production furnaces. The charcoal-fired industry of the past was rapidly replaced.

The greatest concentration of iron production was in Merthyr Tydfil where four massive works grew up – Dowlais, Cyfarthfa, Penydarren and Plymouth. And as iron replaced copper as the leading metal industry in Wales so Merthyr Tydfil replaced Swansea as the largest town in the country. In 1801 Merthyr's population had grown to more than seven thousand and the town maintained its lead for sixty years, attracting a steady flow of people to work in the numerous ironworks which opened in the area.

10

Francis Crawshay was the Ironworks Manager at the Hirwaun Ironworks north of Aberdare and the Trefforest Tinplate Works

David Davies, Fineries, Hirwaun.

John Davies was the Tin Mills Manager at Hirwaun.

Another David Davies was a Cinder Filler at the Hirwaun Works.

Llewellyn Jenkins, employed as Foreman Carpenter at Hirwaun.

Rees Davies, was employed as an engineer at Hirwaun, as his roll of drawings and dividers suggests.

Thomas Francis, carrying sticks of dynamite, was a quarryman working at the Trefforest Works.

David Lewis' job was the Storekeeper at Hirwaun.

John Llewellyn was the Foreman Smith at Trefforest.

David Williams worked as a Carpenter at Trefforest.

near Pontypridd. 'Mr Frank' as he was known to his workers, was the second son of the Cyfarthfa ironmaster William Crawshay II. Considered idle and eccentric by his father, Francis was not a typical ironmaster. He was close friends with the colouful political radical Dr William Price, who saved his wife Laura Crawshay's life by performing a caesaraen section. He loved sailing his steam yacht to France and seems to have been more interested in the people who worked for him, than in making a profit for the company. He removed the truck system at his works, established two schools and when cholera struck he was reported to have left money in a stream, to avoid infection, for the families of those who had died. He was popular with his workers as he was the only member of the Crawshays who could speak Welsh fluently.

Around 1835 Francis commissioned portraits of a selection of his employees, which was highly unusual for the time. These realistic paintings show how many different occupations there were in the iron and tin industry. When the pictures were remounted in the 1920s each was found to have a label detailing the name, place of work and job of the sitter.

One of them shows David Davies (top left) who worked in the Finery at Hirwaun. This was where the carbon content of cast pig iron was reduced so that the iron was not too brittle to be made into tin plate. The cast iron was re-melted and stirred in a puddling furnace. David is holding a long iron pole called a rabble, which he used to 'puddle' the metal. When the metal began to melt, he would watch carefully until it was ready to be divided into separate balls called 'puddle rolls'. At just the right moment he would collect the white hot lumps of iron with his rabble and then haul them out of the furnace and give them to the Shingler. The Shingler used a steam hammer to form the iron into small oblong blocks called 'blooms' which could then be rolled into strips or sheets of wrought iron in the rolling mill. The iron which David helped to produce was made into sheet iron and rails, which were exported to construct railways as far away as Russia and America. Both products helped the British Empire expand.

'Gentlemen puddlers' like David were well paid for this skilled and dangerous work. But many puddlers died young and life expectancy generally for ironworkers in Merthyr was only seventeen years. David had lost an eye and many puddlers' found their eyesight was ruined through working so close to the furnaces, making their working life short lived. The census of 1851 shows David Davies lived in Big Row in Merthyr with his wife and four children, sharing their home with a nephew and a lodger.

Women and children also worked at the Trefforest works.

Family feuds and industrial secrets

Around 1700 a Pontypool ironmaster, John Hanbury, became the first person in Britain to develop a rolling mill to make galvanised metal known as tinplate. Heated iron bars were rolled several times to make smooth, thin sheets of iron that were then dipped in molten tin. A sizeable tinplate industry developed around Ponypool and Caerleon (surviving in Caerleon until the late nineteenth century and Pontypool until the 1960s).

About the same time a manager at Hanbury's ironworks, Thomas Allgood, discovered a way of coating tinplate to produce a hard lacquered surface, similar to the Japanware which Dutch traders brought to Europe from Japan. His sons, Edward and John, developed the technique setting up a cottage business producing decorative japanware and employing specialist craftsmen.

Japanware was the height of fashion and the Allgood's kept their japanning method a secret. Before Edward's death he passed the process to his three sons and nephew, but they quarrelled over access to it and two of his sons, Thomas and Edward, set up a rival factory in Usk. The family feud ran deep. Many of the skilled workers, including the company's main artist and the company's financers moved to Usk. Agents sold their japanware in London's fashionable shops.

John Allgood and his cousin Thomas found new financial backers for the Pontypool company, which also prospered, even exporting japanware to America. Competition between the two firms was intense. *'The articles from the rival manufactory in Usk are decidedly superior in design and finish, and are generally a rich chocolate brown, ornamented with a profusion of tiny gold stars, gold flowers or gold butterflies'*, wrote the Pontypool Free Press. Japanware made in Pontypool graced the tables of King Louis XVIII and Catherine the Great. Years after the factories had closed, local people were still called Pontypool or Usk Butterflies, harking back to the butterfly motifs which had decorated local japanware.

15

Women employed at the Midland Metal Spinners' Tea Pot Works in Neath in the 1950s. This was probably a public relation photo; most work in the tinplate industry was unpleasant, dirty and dangerous.

Tin-opolis

The first tinplate works in west Wales were established in the Swansea Valley near Clydach in 1745. By the late nineteenth century so many people were employed in the tin industry along the coast at Llanelli, coating thin sheets of iron with tin to produce tinplate, that the area had become known as 'Tin-opolis'. Jobs here had appropriately descriptive names: the Rollerman passed the plates through the rolls and screwed down the gap between the rolls, the Doubler folded the sheets, the Behinder took the plates over the mill back to the Rollerman and First and Second Helpers 'helped'. This was hot, noisy and smelly work, and injury and burns were so common that the average age of death for these men was forty-five. Injured men, boys and women were employed to separate the plates and clean them.

Tinplate was the plastic of the nineteenth century and one of its most significant uses was to preserve perishable food stuffs in cans. For nearly three hundred years the tinplate produced in Llanelli was used to can everything from sardines to syrup. Before mechanisation, can manufacture was highly labour intensive. A skilled craftsman could make just one hundred and fifty cans in a twelve hour day. But the expansion of the south Wales tinplate industry halted in the 1880s due to competition from America. Up until this time Wales had produced ninety percent of the world's tinplate.

Steel plate took over from iron after C. W. Siemens rolled the first steel in 1875 at the Llandore works near Swansea. The tradition of working metals into manufactures in this area continued well into the 20th century. In the 1930s the Felinfoel Brewery in Llanelli became the first brewery in Britain to can beer, just beating their rival Buckley Brewery. Local tin-plate manufacturer Metal Box supplied the cans and despite looking like tins of metal polish the beer can soon caught on.

Iron capital

By 1845 the Dowlais Ironworks, which employed more than seven thousand people was the largest ironworks in the world. The Dowlais ironmaster Josiah John Guest (1785 – 1852), had become Merthyr's first Member of Parliament in 1832. His wife Charlotte, the daughter of an English earl, was one of the most influential figures in nineteenth century Welsh cultural history. Living in Dowlais overlooking the massive ironworks, an area that was predominantly Welsh speaking, she learnt Welsh and translated the medieval Welsh tales of the Mabinogion into English.

In many respects the Guests were philanthropists, recognising the need for mass education, establishing schools and introducing new teaching methods. After the Chartist demonstration in London of 1848 Charlotte wrote, *'I know we cannot make people good and religious by Act of Parliament. The first step is to make them comfortable and happy.'*

But the Guests appear to have been blind to the deplorable sanitation and housing their workers endured. They were not alone. Few of Merthyr's industrialists wanted to pay to clean up the town or invest in public health. E.F. Roberts visited Dowlais in 1852 and wrote, *'.....the disgusting aspect of the whole made me marvel that in the neighbourhood of the largest works in the country, perhaps the world.... the apathy of proprietorship could be so great as to neglect the drainage facilities'.*

Charlotte took over the Dowlais works when her husband became ill and she became owner after his death in 1852. What some considered a scandalous marriage followed in 1855 when she married her son's tutor who was only twenty-eight. She was forty-three. Together they travelled across Europe, meeting up with the Merthyr painter Penry Williams, who was living and working in Italy, and indulging in the Victorian fashion for collecting things.

▶ Lady Charlotte Guest (1812 – 1895) who kept a diary for nearly seventy years documenting both family life (she had ten children in thirteen years) and events in the wider world.

19

⌃ Miner with tram, Rhondda.

◁ One-armed Haulier Iwan Deveraux
worked at Tower Colliery in the 1920s.
The possibility of injury at work was
ever present. If you lost a limb in an
accident or colliery explosion there was
little choice but to continue working to
keep food on the table.

Down the pit

In the coal industry there were many different occupations, both underground and at the surface. In the early years collieries employed Patchworkers to dig for coal and other minerals straight from the hillside, a practice which left scars called 'patches' littered across the landscape. Until 1842 children were employed as Trappers or Door-keepers, opening and closing doors along the underground roads, helping to control the mine ventilation system. Many young children lost fingers, or worse. Commissioners for the Children's Employment Report in 1842 found eleven and twelve year old Mary and Rachel Enoch working as door-keepers: *'We leave the house before six each morning and are in the level until seven o'clock and sometimes later...Rachel ... was run over by a tram a while ago and was home ill a long time.'*

Most boys aged between eight and twelve were Trammers who pushed and pulled the trams, which were wheeled carts or barrows used to move the coal. The Mines Act of 1842 banned women and boys under ten from working underground, but not above ground, creating plenty of scope for the Act to be ignored, especially as workers didn't want to see their incomes reduced.

A much more significant set of reforms came with the 1872 Mines Act which introduced a clear management structure to ensure safe disciplined mining operations. Up until this Act each team of colliers was led by a gang master known as a 'butty', who contracted work and collected the pay. The 'butty' was, in effect, a middle man who negotiated between the mine owner and miners. The Act abolished the butty system and also introduced training and certification for managers. It was a landmark development in the coal industry and most of the jobs described below were created as a direct result of the changed management structure.

An Overman was a management official who oversaw the work of miners. The Foreman was responsible for safety at the coal face and checked for gas. A Ripper was employed to rip away the roof and floor of a coal seam so that there was enough height to bring horses up to the coal face. A Roadman's job was to maintain the underground roadways. At the surface a Winding Man drove the engine which hauled the cages up and down the mine shaft. A Pump Engineman prevented the mines from flooding. Lampmen kitted miners out with lights and ensured they all returned safely to the surface. Blacksmiths made and repaired tools and equipment. The miner's tools - a pick and shovel - were precious possessions. At the end of the shift they would put the tools on the bar where they were locked for safety. If they were taken home, then a strike was imminent.

The Company Check Weigher weighed the coal in the drams to calculate miners' wages. Another Check Weigher was employed to do the same job again, paid by the miners who wanted to ensure true records were kept. Disabled men and young boys were employed to pick out stones and rubbish from the coal.

As the mines became deeper and longer the transportation systems changed. An Ostler looked after the horses which were kept underground whilst Hauliers drove the horse and tram from the coal face to the heart of the mine. There were other jobs away from the coalfield in the coastal ports. Coal Trimmers were employed in the docks to ensure ships were correctly loaded with coal cargos, so that they were stable at sea.

22

∧ Stokers at Bwllfa Colliery.

< Boys waiting to go down Penrikyber Colliery in the 1920s.

Jobs for the girls

Women worked alongside men in both the iron and coal industries, doing heavy manual tasks, but often paid less for doing exactly the same job. Huge amounts of waste material – slag and ash – produced by the blast furnaces had to be disposed of and women and girls were employed to dump hot ash and slag on enormous tips close to the ironworks. These Tip Girls worked outside, often bare foot, in all weathers all year round. They played a vital role in the iron industry, but existed at the very bottom of society.

Many women were employed in the pits as Haulers or Trammers, dragging trams laden with coal along tramways. This 'horse work' wrecked their bodies. A young girl talking to the Employment Commissioners in 1842 told them, *'I draw the drams (carts).... The mine is wet where we work as the water passes through the roof and the workings are only 30 – 33 inches high. I have been laid idle for two months, as a horse fell on me and crushed my inside'.*

Worse still, there were many deaths amongst women employed as Tram Oilers or Greasers, who were struck or run over by the trams they were working on. A seven year old girl from Swansea, Mary Price, was killed in 1855 when a tram ran her over at a mine. Mary Rees a twenty-one year old Greaser from Aberdare died in 1887 when she was hit by a tram on her way

◀ A servant girl, photographed by John Thomas around 1875.

▶ This tip girl worked at the Dowlais Ironworks. A contemporary writer described the tip girls as, *'Bold eyed yet squalidly picturesque, with cheap earrings and coloured kerchief'.*

to collect her wages from the works office. Many more women died when their clothing became caught in machinery. Margaretta Edwards a Dressing Girl working for the Wye Valley Mining Company died on a windy day in December 1875 when her clothing was blown into the crushing machinery, dragging her in and crushing her. Jane Jenkins, a fourteen year old Oil Girl working for Guest and Co at the Dowlais Colliery in Merthyr Tydfil, died in 1866 when she became entangled with a carriage at the pit top.

Women and children also worked at the surface collecting and sorting coal on the tips. This work became increasingly important after the Mines Act of 1842 prohibited women and children from working underground and they had to find new ways of making a living. Domestic service became the largest occupation for women.

Even women who didn't work in the mines found their lives revolved around coal. Heating water to fill a tin bath for coal-blackened husbands and sons wasn't just hard work, it was dangerous and it wasn't unheard of for young children to die after falling into a bath of boiling water. Elizabeth Andrews (1882 – 1960), the daughter of a miner from Hirwaun, fought for years for pit-head baths to be installed. Elizabeth, who had been a suffragette, gave evidence to the Sankey Commission in Parliament in 1918, describing women as 'nothing but slaves'. Probably more women died of overwork, tuberculosis, and childbirth than miners were killed at work.

26

⌃ Girls as young as twelve and thirteen were sent away 'in service', to work as servants for the families of industrialists and the wealthy middle classes.

« Women working at the Bwllfa Colliery, 1870.

‹ Miner's bath time – it wasn't until 1950 that every mine had pithead baths.

The chemistry of progress

Chemists were employed in many iron and steel companies, playing a significant role as ironmasters sought to keep up with rapid technological change. After its invention in 1856 Henry Bessemer's method for converting iron into steel was quickly adopted in south Wales. Steel, which was stronger than iron, was becoming a more valuable product, but many local iron ores used to make iron contained impurities such as phosphorus, which made brittle steel.

Sidney Gilchrist Thomas who had studied metallurgy at the University of London, believed he could make his fortune if he invented a process to remove unwanted phosphorus. His cousin, Percy Carlyle Gilchrist was employed as the Work's Chemist for the Blaenavon Ironworks Company. The two cousins experimented at weekends in an improvised laboratory in Blaenavon, perfecting Sidney's technique for removing phosphorus. By 1878 the Blaenavon Iron Company was supporting their work and the technique soon caught on, being used in ironworks as far away as Russia by the early 1880s.

The cousins' discovery did more to assist steelmaking in America and Germany where phosphoric ore was common. When the American steelmaker Andrew Carnegie bought the rights to use the process in America he paid them two hundred and fifty thousand dollars saying, *'These two young men, Thomas and Gilchrist of Blaenavon, did more for Britain's greatness than all the Kings and Queens put together.'* Unfortunately Sidney didn't live long enough to enjoy the rewards as he died in 1885 when he was just thirty-four, his lungs damaged by the fumes from his experiments.

The need to protect new inventions created new jobs. Rhys Jenkins (1859 – 1953) from Mountain Ash became one of the first Patent Examiners in 1884 at the reformed Patent Office. An avid collector of engineering history over sixty years, his collection is now in the Science Museum Library in London.

To Russia with love

By the middle of the nineteenth century a number of men from south Wales were launching careers as international entrepreneurs. In 1870 a hundred skilled miners and specialist ironworkers, along with eight ships loaded with equipment, left Britain for Imperial Russia. Most of the men were from south Wales, particularly Merthyr Tydfil and they were led by a Merthyr – born engineer John Hughes who had started his career at the Cyfarthfa Ironworks where his father worked.

South Wales led the world in industrial expertise and it was here that Imperial Russia looked for skilled engineers and managers when it wanted to develop its own industry and railways. With the UK iron trade depressed in the 1860s and 1870s Hughes found it easy to recruit skilled workers from the Valleys.

Their voyage took them through the Mediterranean and the Black Sea to the Sea of Azov and then by bullock cart for

◄ John Hughes (c. 1815 – 1889) who left a fortune of over £90,000 when he died in St Petersburg.

29

seventy miles to the site on the Ukrainian steppe where Hughes had bought a concession to establish a metal plant and factory to produce rails. Disease and severe winter weather didn't stop Hughes and his team building a blast furnace in only eight months. His New Russia Company produced its first rails in 1873 and the works became the largest in Russia, employing twelve thousand people.

Developing into a large industrial complex as more engineering and technical staff came from Wales, the town which grew up around the works was called Hughesovka (now Donetz). There was a large expatriate community and they even imported a pack of hunting hounds from the Court Estate in Merthyr Tydfil. There was a steady flow of people between Wales and Russia. Some made the lengthy journey many times and links with home remained strong. When children were starving in Merthyr Tydfil in 1877, men working for the New Russia Company gave over £50 to a charity fund to send back home.

America calling

Scientists took their expertise to the New World too. *'Probably no man has done more for the permanent prosperity of the United States than Mr. Thomas, and his efforts of enterprise entitle him to a distinguished place among America's useful citizens'*, wrote a New York magazine in 1869. Mr. Thomas was David Thomas, who produced the world's first anthracite iron at the Ynyscedwyn Ironworks in the Swansea Valley. He was 'head hunted' to work in America, establishing the Thomas Iron Company, the largest producer of anthracite iron in the United States.

◀ Amelia and Elizabeth Lethbridge with their father William. Wearing black, they had recently returned to Hughesovka after burying their mother in Swansea.

31

Boat number 502 heading north from Cardiff on the Glamorganshire Canal in the 1920s.

A view of Castell Coch, Tongwynlais, from the banks of the Glamorganshire Canal at the end of the 19th century.

Canny canal engineers

The iron industry developed where its raw materials - ironstone, limestone and coal - were found in a strip along the Heads of the Valleys bordering the Brecon Beacons. Roads were so poor that transporting finished iron goods to customers and the coastal ports was a hazardous process. Teams of packhorses were linked together to carry iron from Merthyr Tydfil to Cardiff – a journey that could take three days. Even in good conditions a pack horse could only carry a fifth of a ton and in winter most roads in the Valleys were impassable. An alternative way of moving goods had to be found. A canal barge, laden with twenty-five tons, could be pulled by one horse at a speed of about two miles an hour, although the state of the water supply in the canal could slow down the rate of travel.

An English ironmaster Francis Homfray, who opened the Penydarren Ironworks in Merthyr Tydfil in 1782, had seen the Staffordshire and Worcestershire canal being built. He knew a canal engineer who had worked on this canal and invited him to engineer the first major canal in Wales, the Glamorganshire, which would run nearly twenty-five miles from Merthyr Tydfil to Cardiff.

Three Thomas's - Thomas Dadford senior, his son (also called Thomas) and a colleague, Thomas Sheasby - were engaged to engineer the canal, starting work in Merthyr Tydfil in August 1790. The first boat arrived in Cardiff four years later in February 1794. It now took only two days for a canal boat to travel from Merthyr Tydfil to Cardiff.

Canal mania ensured plenty of speculative investors. At least two thirds of the investment was raised in London, although it was Richard Crawshay, ironmaster of the Cyfarthfa Ironworks, who became the main mover behind the canal. He wrote in 1797, *'My Canal commences at my Door down to the Sea Lock at Cardiff....our boats carry about 25 Tons and are attended by a little welch horse & 2 Men.'*

The 'three Thomas's' had engineered a route with fifty locks at a cost of over £100,000, but the canal trade boomed and investors soon made embarassingly large profits. In 1806 directors decided to repay 20% of the tolls users had paid. Profits continued to grow and by 1815 charges were actually reduced. This had the effect of increasing profits again as even more traffic used the canal! In 1833 lighting was installed to enable night-time traffic along the canal and Sunday working was also allowed. By 1840 two hundred boats or more were working the canal.

The men and women who worked the privately owned boats up and down the canals, from the iron works and collieries through the locks to the ports at Cardiff, Newport and Swansea were called Bargees or Hobblers. They paid a toll, per ton, per mile to the canal company, the rate depending on what they were carrying. The canal companies acted as toll collectors and managed canal operations through a Clerk. Each boat had to be in the hands of a capable Boatman and a Haulier who had to remain with the horse all the time.

Whole communities lived on and alongside the canals, including the Lock Keepers and Length Men who had canal-side cottages and were responsible for checking and protecting the condition

of the canal. The canal companies employed a team of craftsmen to carry out the maintenance work. There were even Canal Police, who were appointed when pilfering from the canal boats became too much of a problem. Pubs and stabling for the horses developed alongside the canal. The Canal House in Merthyr was a traditional boatman's pub with a brew house alongside.

The canals were built at astonishing speed by sub-contractors, who worked under the direction of the Company Engineer. They employed gangs of labourers called Navigators or Navvies to excavate the route, and teams of Masons and Carpenters to construct the locks, bridges, aqueducts and tunnels. Thomas Dadford senior had started his working life as a carpenter on the canals.

Much to the annoyance of local farmers, better wages enticed labourers away from the land. When the canals were superseded by the railways, many transferred their construction skills to railway building. The Monmouthshire Canal Company converted to building railways alongside its canal in 1845, and even built over closed down sections of the canal at Pontypool and Newport. But it wasn't just the railways which led to the decline of the canals. Subsidence from mining caused serious problems, especially on the Aberdare Canal, where in numerous places the towpaths were flooded and horses and boatmen had to wade through water.

◄ Unloading a boat on the Glamorgan Canal.

► A fire boat called The 'Fire Queen' worked on the Glamorganshire Canal in the centre of Cardiff.

Water fights

There always seemed to be conflict surrounding the canals: boardroom battles, fights between the navvies and disputes over water resources. Water was one of the most valuable commodities of the Industrial Revolution. Disagreement over water supplies to the Glamorgan Canal and the Plymouth Ironworks in Merthyr caused a dispute between two ironmasters, Richard Hill and Richard Crawshay, which resulted in lengthy litigation and large legal fees. A letter written to Crawshay in 1812 illustrates how precarious the water supply was to the Canal. *'The Rain in the Hills this morning has given us Water to fill the canal from Merthyr... but I am fearful it will be of short duration. It will however enable us to take a trip of Iron down from Cyfarthfa.'*

Proposals to improve the docks at Cardiff where the Glamorganshire Canal ended caused alarm to local iron manager Richard Blakemore. He secured an injunction to stop the canal company, concerned that the proposals would affect water supplies to his works at Melingriffith. The Marquess of Bute also opposed the scheme, claiming that his fishery would be affected if water was extracted for the new scheme. He drew up plans to build a new dock himself – the West Bute Dock.

King of the rails

South Wales began attracting some of the best engineers and inventors in the world - men who wanted to work where the opportunities were. A Cornishman, Richard Trevithick (1771 – 1833), had the idea of putting a steam engine on to rails. He came to Merthyr Tydfil to settle a five hundred guinea bet between two Merthyr ironmasters, Samuel Homfray and Richard Crawshay. Homfray wanted to prove that Trevithick could build a steam engine that would haul ten tons of iron along nine miles of tramway from Penydarren to Quaker's Yard.

On 12th February 1804 five wagons loaded with ten tons of iron and seventy passengers were pulled by Trevithick's steam engine along the tramway at a speed of five miles an hour. Trevithick's invention worked. This was twenty-five years before Stephenson's famous train, The Rocket, but no one took up Trevithick's idea - his engine was so heavy it broke the rails and its boiler was large and inefficient. He died penniless.

Tramways filled a gap in the transport system, reaching the places the canals couldn't, and they became an integral part of the network. The early tramways were built by ironmasters and landowners. The horses needed to pull the trams along the rails were more often owned by farmers, who became dependant on tramway contracts for their livelihood.

These horses are operating on the Sirhowy Valley Tramroad which ran from the Sirhowy Ironworks to Newport. They are crossing an impressive new stone bridge across the river at Risca, built by the Sirhowy Tramroad Company. c.1810.

The railways revolutionised industrial transport, linking together mines, docks, towns and factories. Canal barges had taken two days to travel between Merthyr and Cardiff. Steam engines on the Taff Vale Railway, which opened in 1841, could travel the same distance pulling heavier loads, in just over an hour. The Taff Vale Railway paved the way for the opening up of the Rhondda Valleys and the rush for 'black gold' during the 'Klondike' period of coal production in the second half of the nineteenth century. A huge shunting yard was established at Pontypool, which distributed the coal from south Wales to places all over England, and a railway community grew up alongside at Griffithstown. New railway connections also allowed new ports such as Barry, to open along the coast.

The railway companies employed Labourers, Mechanics, Pointsmen and their own Policemen. They also created thousands of jobs in the iron and coal industry: railways needed rails, which the ironworks of south Wales excelled in producing for an international market, whilst coal was in demand to run the new steam engines.

Unlike the canals which followed the contours of the valleys, railways had to cross the deep river valleys of south Wales. The engineers' solution was to construct impressive viaducts and bridges which became a feature of the new industrial landscape. Described as *'one of the most significant examples of technological achievement during the Industrial Revolution'*, the Crumlin Viaduct on the Newport, Abergavenny and Hereford Railway had to be tested before it could be used by the public. A courageous volunteer was recruited to drive a train over the bridge for the very first time. Local folklore recalls how the volunteer, a gentleman from Pontypool known as 'Mad Jack', calmed his nerves before the test by visiting all the pubs in Crumlin. He drove the train at top speed across the viaduct, forgetting the engineer's instructions to make the crossing slowly saying, *'When eternity looks you in the face, you may as well go at full speed to meet it!'*

38

⌃ Railway navvies on
the Blaencwm Tunnel.

‹ The Crumlin Viaduct
on the Newport,
Abergavenny and
Hereford railway
extension to Taff Vale.

Engineers played a crucial role in bringing new innovations to south Wales. William Williams, an Engineer employed at the Cyfarthfa Ironworks in Merthyr Tydfil, clearly enjoyed the good life as he was very overweight and had to be moved around the Ironworks on a trolley made especially for him!

Feats of engineering fantasy

Pioneering bridge builders conquered the challenging terrain of the Valleys with feats of engineering fantasy. When William Edwards (1738 – 1816) completed Pontypridd's Old Bridge over the Taff in 1756 it was the largest single span bridge in the United Kingdom. But it would have meant much more to William as his father had drowned trying to ford the River Taff on horseback.

At the turn of the twentieth century the French bridge engineer, Ferdinand Arnodin was chosen to design a new crossing over the River Usk in Newport, a town which had grown rapidly from just over 1000 people in 1801 to 62,000 in 1901. Divided by a river with one of the highest tidal ranges in the world, Ferdinand's Flying Ferry' was an engineering triumph – the Newport Transporter Bridge. Completed in 1906 at a cost of £98,000, the aerial ferry ensured that ships still had clear passage up the Usk, whilst the transporter 'gondola' carried goods and people across the river to the Orb Steelworks on the east bank.

Travellers compared Pontypridd's new bridge with the Rialto in Venice. Its spectacular single arch established William Edwards' reputation as a bridge builder – pictured here around 1779

Marvellous men in their flying machines

Two aviators from south Wales – Charles Rolls and Ernest Willows – were setting the pace in aeronautics. The motoring and aviation pioneer Charles Rolls (1877 – 1910) from Monmouth, was a Cambridge engineering graduate whose partnership with Frederick Royce created the world famous car manufacturer Rolls-Royce, a company still synonymous with luxury cars and aero-engineering.

In 1908 Wilbur Wright, one of the famous Wright brothers, took Charles on a five minute flight which changed his life. He became a founding member of the Royal Aero Club, restoring some of Britain's prestige in the air when he made the first non-stop double crossing of the English Channel on 2nd June 1910, shortly before his death in a flying accident. He has the dubious fame of being the first person in Britain to die in an air crash.

A similar fate lay in store for pioneering aviation engineer Ernest Thompson Willows (1896 – 1926). Shortly before Roll's death a £50 prize was offered to the first aviator to fly across Cardiff. Willows took up the challenge on June 4th 1910, flying from his hangar and workshop in Pengam Moors, Splott and landing in

« Charles Rolls, with Wilbur Wright at the controls, in France 1908. This was Rolls' first flight in a plane, and he wrote shortly afterwards, *'The power of flight.... is destined to work great change in human life as we know it today'*.

‹ Charles Rolls in his study.

43

front of crowds at City Hall. In August 1910 he flew from Cardiff to London, having to fly low and shout for directions on several occasions! Later that year he became the first person to fly across the English Channel in his yellow cigar-shaped 'City of Cardiff' airship.

The self-taught Willows established the Willows Aircraft Company in Cardiff (rather than follow his father into dentistry!). Spectacularly showing off the improvements he had engineered to airship control and manoeuvrability, he flew his airship around the Eiffel Tower in January 1911. He went on to supply airships to the War Office and his designs were later developed into the blimp airship. He was only 40 when he died in a ballooning accident in 1926.

E. T. Willows preparing to land outside City Hall, Cardiff in 1910.

E. T. Willows after his flight from Cardiff to London, 1910.

45

Money, money, money...

Where did the money come from to build ironworks and dig canals, invest in railways and sink deep mines? Huge sums were needed: £100,000 had been invested at the Cyfarthfa Ironworks alone by the end of the nineteenth century. Wealthy entrepreneurs from England had the necessary capital to invest and settled in south Wales. One of them, Richard Crawshay established the Crawshay Dynasty who became one of the most influential families in Wales, owning a vast iron empire.

Richard Crawshay (1739 – 1810) was a farmer's son from Yorkshire who ran away to London when he was sixteen. He worked his way up to become one of the wealthiest merchants in the city. One of his business associates, Anthony Bacon, established the Cyfarthfa Ironworks in 1767. Both men had made money from trade connected with slave plantations such as tobacco and guns. When Bacon died in 1786 Richard took over the Cyfarthfa Ironworks in Merthyr Tydfil. One of the most successful industrialists ever, he turned the Cyfarthfa Works into the largest in the world at the time, producing cannons and cannonballs for the Navy. Nelson came to meet Crawshay when he toured Wales in 1802. To mark the visit cannons and guns were fired and a young boy was accidentally killed, much to the

◀ Richard Crawshay played a major role in the development of the Glamorgan Canal, recognising that improved transport to Cardiff would make him even wealthier. He was, probably, the world's first millionaire leaving £1.5 million.

▶ Laura Crawshay – wife of Francis Crawshay.

distress of Nelson's mistress, Lady Emma Hamilton, who gave eight guineas for the boy's funeral.

William Crawshay I (1764 – 1834) inherited a complex business empire with many partners. With his eldest son William Crawshay II, he managed to maintain Cyfarthfa's role as the world's leading iron producer.

William Crawshay II (1788 – 1867) carried on the Cyfarthfa Works, often wrangling with his father over the best way of running their empire. He spent £30,000 on Cyfarthfa Castle which he built overlooking the ironworks in 1825, a venture which caused bitter argument with his father who thought it an extravagant folly. Despite having fifteen children his life was blighted by sadness. He lost two wives and his eldest son William III drowned crossing the Severn Estuary. He gave the works to his eldest son by his second wife, Robert Thompson Crawshay, passing over Francis Crawshay who was next in line, but considered idle and eccentric.

Robert Thompson Crawshay (1812 – 1879) managed Cyfarthfa, whilst his half brothers Francis and Henry managed the works in Hirwaun and Trefforest. Robert's great passion was music and he set up the Cyfarthfa Brass Band in 1838, employing professional players from England to ensure his band was the best. An edition of the Household Words magazine published in 1860 reported that, *'The correspondent of a leading London newspaper, while visiting Merthyr, was exceedingly surprised by hearing boys in the Cyfarthfa Works whistling arias rarely heard except in the fashionable ball room, opera house or drawing room. He afterwards discovered that the proprietor of the Works, Mr. Robert Crawshay, had established among his men a brass band, which practices once a week throughout the year.'*

Robert married Rose Mary Yeates in 1846. One of the work's rolling sheds was converted into a huge banquet hall to celebrate their wedding and on their return from honeymoon a team of Crawshay workers unhitched the horses and hauled their carriage the last three miles back to Cyfarthfa Castle. An ambitious lady who championed women's rights, Rose Crawshay often took into service at the Castle women who had fallen on hard times. She also set up a soup kitchen ensuring no food from Cyfarthfa was wasted. Family life deteriorated when Robert suffered a stroke and went deaf and eventually Rose chose to live in London.

No longer able to enjoy his band's music Robert took up photography. He built a studio in the Castle and a travelling hut which he could take out into the Brecon Beacons. His daughter Rose Harriet was his favourite subject and he made her pose in weird and wonderful outfits. She wrote in her diary in 1868, *'Papa came in with the ugliest, dirtiest, nastiest old straw bonnet that ever existed and a cap (thank goodness that was clean) for me to be photographed in as a fish woman.'*

Robert refused to convert from iron to the more popular steel. By 1874 the Cyfarthfa Works had closed. After his death in 1879 one of Robert's sons, William Thompson Crawshay (1847 – 1918), spent £150,000 converting the Cyfarthfa site to steel production, only for it to be bought out by Guest Keen Nettleford in 1902 and closed in 1910.

48

◀ William Crawshay II.

🔳 Robert Thompson Crawshay.

▶ Rose Harriet Crawshay. Robert never forgave his daughter when she married and he disinherited her children. On his grave he asked for three words -'God Forgive Me'.

Artistic artisans

There was much appreciation of the arts amongst the middle and upper classes in Merthyr at this time and artists were often commissioned to paint the movers and shakers of industry. Ironmasters, coal owners and engineers, as well as their families and the places they lived, became the subject of numerous portraits and landscape paintings. Several Merthyr artists managed to escape from industrial jobs at Cyfarthfa and Dowlais and lead artistic lives.

One of the best known international artists of the 19th century, Penry Williams (1798 – 1885), was the son of a Merthyr house decorator. It's likely that he worked in the drawing office at Cyfarthfa and was sent to the Royal Academy in 1822, possibly by William Crawshay II or Sir John Josiah Guest. Penry had painted a picture of the industrial unrest at Merthyr in 1816, which probably brought him to the attention of the Guests and Crawshays who commissioned him on several occasions. He spent most of his later life painting in Rome.

Another artist, Thomas Prytherch, started work at the Dowlais Iron Works where his father worked, when he was ten. By the time he was twenty his drawing talents had been recognised and he was employed as an engineering draftsman. Local patronage enabled him to attend art college and travel to Antwerp to study.

Many industrialists supported local painters. In this painting titled *Industrial Landscape*, Penry Williams probably includes the people who commissioned the picture – two people on horseback, enjoying the parkland setting around the Bute Ironworks.

Coal tycoons!

To begin with coal mines were small – either 'drift' mines which were tunnels into the hillside, or shallow opencast 'patches' where coal was near the surface – and these were developed mainly by local people. As the mines got deeper the cost of investment increased. New pits needed new money – which came from prosperous families or groups of men who raised capital by setting up a limited company. Unlike iron, coal offered opportunities to Welsh entrepreneurs, and men such as Thomas Phillips, Thomas Protheroe and Thomas Powell invested in the Monmouthshire Valleys in the early nineteenth century. The buildings and equipment at a colliery belonged to the coal owners, whilst the land the collieries were sunk on belonged to landlords who became extremely rich from the mineral royalties (known as galeage) which were paid per ton. By the end of the nineteenth century four very large, powerful companies controlled most of the coal industry in south Wales.

Many of the coal owners lived outside the mining communities they controlled, on country estates remote from the people who made their money. Most were hated and despised. David Alfred Thomas, Baron Rhondda (1856 – 1918) controlled the Cambrian Combine collieries in Monmouthshire and the Rhondda. Thomas Powell (1779 – 1863) opened collieries in the Rhymney and Aberdare Valleys, becoming one of the largest coal exporters in the world. After his death the Powell Duffryn Steam Coal Company Ltd (P & D) was established, soon known by another name – Poverty and Death.

William Thomas Lewis (1837 – 1914), Lord Merthyr led the Lewis Merthyr Consolidated Collieries Ltd in the Aber Valley, Porth and Pontypridd. He was a mining engineer who became manager of Lord Bute's mineral assets when he was only twenty-seven, making him one of the most powerful men in Welsh industry. The coal owners had their own association, the South Wales Coal Owners' Association, which Lord Merthyr helped establish in 1872. Representing eighty-five companies who between them owned two hundred and twenty pits, the Association was a powerful force, united in opposition to wage increases and claims for compensation.

There were notable exceptions, men who used their wealth and influence to provide schools, hospitals, libraries and chapels. One of these was David Davies, known to his men as 'Davies yr Ocean'. He built some of the early railways in mid Wales, generating enough capital to invest in the coal industry in south Wales. Taking out a lease from the Crawshay family on land near Treorchy, Davies and his workers looked for coal for over a year before striking black gold at the Cwmparc Mine, just days before his funds ran out. His Ocean Coal Company was soon employing over five thousand men.

Davies' greatest achievement was the construction of Barry Docks at a cost of £2 million in 1889, which solved both high charges on the Taff Vale Railway and congestion at the Bute Docks in Cardiff. Both the Taff Vale Railway Company and the Bute family opposed this new port. The railway stood to loose coal trade whilst the Butes controlled Cardiff Docks through which Rhondda coal had previously been exported. The hamlet of Barry soon became a busy dock town.

From a Calvinistic Methodist family, Davies was teetotal, a strict observer of the Sabbath with a strong sense of philanthropic duty. This didn't stop him making money. When he died in 1890 Ocean Steam and Coal was the largest and most profitable coal company in south Wales. His son Edward took over the businesses but died in 1898. David's granddaughters Gwendoline and Margaret Davies used their inheritance to create one of the best collections of French art in the UK. Also teetotal and Nonconformist, neither sister married, leaving their collections to the National Museum of Wales for everyone to enjoy.

▶ David Davies (1818 – 90), who went from rural rags to riches, becoming the coal magnate behind the Ocean Coal Company and one of Wales' leading industrial entrepreneurs.

52

The richest man in the world

An influential Scottish family, the Butes acquired land across Britain through marriage, moving to Cardiff in 1766 when Lord Mountstuart (the 1st Marquess of Bute) married Charlotte Windsor who owned property in South Wales. At this time Wales didn't have a capital city and Cardiff was only a small town. Using their influence and wealth to invest in the expanding local industries, the Butes helped make Cardiff the greatest coal exporting port in the world.

They also played an instrumental role in building the Glamorgan Canal. Where the Canal ended John, the 2nd Marquess (1793 – 1848), built the Bute Dock in 1839, the first dock on Cardiff's waterfront, at a cost of £350,000. He raised the capital by selling land from his south Wales estates.

The 3rd Marquess John Patrick Crichton Stuart (1847 – 1900) was only six months old when his father died and twelve years old when his mother died. He inherited nearly £500,000 in debts from his father's investment in the Cardiff docks development. But demand for Welsh steam coal, shipped through the docks grew, and the Bute Estate made money from property development in Cardiff. When John came of age in 1868 he was receiving £300,000 a year income from the Estates, making him the richest man in the world.

▶ John Patrick Crichton Stuart, the 3rd Marquess of Bute.

▶▶ A view of the Jubilee Dock, Cardiff around 1849, showing a paddle steamer and a ferry at Bute Dock.

Success brought its own problems. The docks had become so busy and there was so much crime and violence that the 3rd Marquess established the Bute Docks Police Force. But his police force actually added to the crime figures: policemen used swords, were drunk, fell into the docks and were even fined for having snowball fights with customs officers!

Wealth created on the back of industrialisation allowed the Marquess to indulge his passion for architecture, sponsoring many building projects in Cardiff and commissioning the architect and designer William Burges to restore Cardiff Castle and Castell Coch. The Victorians were fascinated by medieval art and architecture and at Castell Coch Bute's and Burges' passion for the romantic was indulged. It took sixteen years to complete the lavish designs, which included a working portculllis and drawbridge. But the castle was never really lived in. The Marquess died in 1900 and the Marchioness and her daughter, Lady Margaret, stayed there for a short time, mourning the loss of a man who had been fascinated by history - one of the great Victorian patrons of the arts and architecture.

55

Hogg medal. 1902.

The head gardener at Cyfarthfa Castle was reputed to have cut a pineapple every day of the year in the 1870s. Industrial wealth bought everything from palaces to pineapples!

Anything money can buy

In 1893 one of the directors of the Great Western Railway, Sir Henry Oakley, acquired Dewstow House overlooking the Severn Estuary near Caldicot. He could enjoy the views over his six hundred acre estate towards the Severn levels where his company's trains steamed east to the Severn Tunnel or west to Newport. Oakley indulged his passion for gardening, creating one of the finest underground grotto gardens in the country, commissioning the fashionable Pulham & Sons who were landscape gardeners to the Queen.

Oakley was just one of many men who made money from the industrialisation of South Wales and spent it in ways which created a legacy for the future. The landscape is littered with evidence of this industrial wealth – castles, parks, follys, civic buildings and engineering masterpieces of the workplace.

Profits from the metal industries built Margam Castle, created for Christopher Rice Mansel Talbot in the 1830s. Talbot demolished the old village of Margam, moving residents to a new settlement so he could have a kitchen garden close to his home. Head gardeners employed at Margam and other estates became important horticulturalists, satisfying the demands of Victorian hosts for exotic food to entertain their guests.

Industrial wealth also created a cultural legacy. A group of well-educated Swansea men established the Royal Institution of South Wales in 1841, for the *'advancement of Science, Literature and the Arts'*. Richard Glynn Vivian (1835 – 1910), also from Swansea, was more interested in the arts than his family's copper business, which he inherited a share of in 1855. He spent a fortune travelling and collecting art. When he lost his sight in 1902 he gave his collection to the City of Swansea who established the Glyn Vivian Art Gallery.

A Butetown family 1950. Tiger Bay was home to many people of Arab, Somali, West African, West Indian and Greek origin.

The Coal Exchange where, in 1907 the first ever £1m cheque was written.

Cosmopolitan Cardiff

For 150 years the global price of coal was set in Cardiff, which became the boom town of late Victorian Britain. Coal merchants would make deals in local pubs, or chalk up the changing price of coal on slates outside their premises. But in 1883 The Coal Exchange in Mount Stuart Square was opened, providing a grand venue for Cardiff's businessmen to meet and make their deals.

By 1910 there were over two hundred and fifty commercial ships for hire in Cardiff and the owners of these 'tramp steamers' met at the Coal Exchange to arrange cargoes of coal to ports around the world. The world's greatest coal exporting port had become so busy that railway style signals were needed to control the flow of shipping!

Returning ships ususally arrived via Liverpool, where crew were discharged and the ships travelled back to Cardiff 'in ballast' with a skeleton crew. The exception was the Baltic trade, where ships returned to Cardiff laden with timber for pit props, the only significant import trade. Sailors made their way overland from other ports to Cardiff where they would 'sign on' to a new ship.

Cardiff was full of men waiting for their next passage. There was even a floating hospital, the Hamadryad Hospital Ship, where seamen could find treatment. A Norwegian Church served as a seamen's mission where sailors could meet. The author Rohl Dahl, was christened at this church. His father was a merchant dealing in the port's timber trade and living in Cardiff.

Sailors from across the world settled close to the docks in an area dubbed 'Tiger Bay', creating a multi-cultural community of many nationalities, especially Somalis, Yeminis, Norwegians, and Chinese. There was always competion for work amongst the sailors and during periods of industrial discontent the dock owners often used Chinese crews originating from overseas, who they knew would accept low wages, to keep the ships sailing. When a crew of Chinese sailors arrived in Cardiff during the seaman's strike of 1911 they suffered physical attack and verbal abuse. At the time there were about two hundred Chinese people living in Cardiff, and there were more than thirty Chinese laundries. Although they had nothing to do with the sailors, every laundry was attacked as hostility towards the Chinese community intensified.

59

▲ Rats running over their beds at night time did little to assist the recovery of patients on the Hamadryad Hospital Ship, which was known as Rat Island.

▶ Described as *'a burly firebrand in the seamen's union'*, 'Captain' Edward Tupper was one of the leaders of the 1911 seamen's strike who addressed strikers at Cardiff's Bute Docks.

Heart ache, health and hope

'People were living in conditions not fit for criminals. No doubt horses, especially race horses were housed better than some of our own citizens are being reared,' wrote Aneurin Bevan. And it was true. The new industrial towns grew so rapidly that their slum conditions provided breeding grounds for disease. Rows of terraced houses crammed many people into a small area, creating public health crises on a scale never seen before. The Rhondda was described as a *'picture of hell. The people are poor creatures, boiling in sweat and dirt, amid their furnaces, pits and rolling mills'.*

Quack doctors and con men offered cures to the gullible. The amazingly named Baron Spolasco of Swansea travelled around South Wales in a grand four horse carriage, setting up shop in local pubs and dispensing bogus cures! He was tried for manslaughter after his medicines allegedly helped kill a girl, but acquitted. However he did serve time for 'evading stamp duty on his medicines'.

It's not surprising that self help societies flourished. Accidents were commonplace in collieries and ironworks and family health was poor. There was no national health service. Few could afford to pay doctors' fees and there was a shortage of medical care. Even in 1914 when the population of the Rhondda was over 180,000 there were only 88 hospital beds.

In Tredegar the Medical Aid Society was set up in 1890 by local miners and steelworkers who decided to club together to employ a doctor. The Society flourished engaging more doctors and nurses, building surgeries and a hospital to provide the residents of Tredegar with comprehensive medical care. Their weekly subscriptions entitled members and their dependants to dental care also. This was unique. Health care found elsewhere

61

◤ Nye Bevan in his home town of Tredegar. Always a rebel he resigned from his cabinet post in 1951 over plans to introduce charges for spectacles and false teeth.

▶ High on the mountainside above Tredegar is Cefn Golau where cholera victims were buried after the 'King of Terrors' struck in 1832, 1849 and 1866. Lime and disinfectants were used to cleanse the town, quack cures were taken, and people turned to religion. A few miles away in Merthyr Lady Charlotte Guest wrote in her diary on 31st July 1849, *'I am sorry to say the accounts of the cholera at Dowlais are fearfully bad.... sometimes upwards of 20 people dying in one day and eight men constantly making coffins.'*

in the Valleys was focused solely on getting men back to work through the Company Doctor – and did not provide for family members or the unemployed.

Health Minister Aneurin Bevan (1897 – 1960) based the National Health Service on his home town's community health scheme, which by the 1920s covered most of Tredegar's population. When the National Health Service was born on 5th July 1948 the government took over responsibility for all medical services. There was free diagnosis and treatment for everyone. The people of Tredegar had been the inspiration for the UK's most respected national institution.

Nye (as he was known) was the fourth child in a family of ten. He started work with his brother William, in the Tytryst Colliery, when he was just fourteen. Nye used the Workmen's Hall and Library in Tredegar, where he and a group of friends set up a discussion group called the Query Club, challenging the influence of the Tredegar Iron and Coal Company which dominated life in the town. This shaped his socialist principles and he became Britain's youngest MP in 1929, winning the Ebbw Vale seat for Labour. The architect of the National Health Service also started the largest public housing programme in Britain.

Miners' lung

Mortality rates were especially high in the mining communities, where 'miners' lung', a dust related disease was endemic. Coal workers' pneumoconiosis was discovered in the late 1930s and by the 1940s the Valleys had the worst coal dust problem in the UK. Fit and previously healthy men were unable to work because of silicosis. In fact miners' trade unions had been campaigning for compensation for dust-damaged miners since the 1920s. Union officials lobbied for more government-funded research and used scientific expertise to strengthen their case.

In 1948 a pioneering doctor, Archie Cochrane, started conducting research in the Rhondda Valleys, recruiting 25,000 people to take part in a survey of chest diseases amongst the mining community. A mobile x-ray machine was parked outside

collieries as part of a mass radiography project. Archie's results helped understanding of the relationship between coal mining and poor health.

Rats were another health hazard. Their urine contaminated underground water with Weil's Disease making rat-catching a vital activity. During lock outs and strikes the rats had to surface to find something to eat, as the steady supply of scraps from miners' food dried up.

A 1945 Picture Post article – The Story of a Miner's Football Team – featured Will Brown, *'formerly a fit member of the Aberpergwm Football Club and a miner from the south west of Wales, who has become totally incapacitated by silicosis, and has been living on compensation for the past two years'.*

205 widows and
542 orphans

A sound dreaded by mothers, wives and children was the continuous wail of the pit hooter. Thousands of men lost their lives in underground explosions and accidents but the small mining community of Senghenydd was struck by tragedy twice. Eighty-two men were lost in a firedamp explosion in May 1901 and in October 1913 another four hundred and thirty-nine men died in the same pit. An explosion, the force of which destroyed the pithead and the winding gear above ground, wiped out a generation underground.

Soon after the disaster a photographer arrived in the village and documented the scene through a series of photographs which appeared in newspapers and on postcards, within days of the tragedy. W. Benton's record provides a moving insight into the human 'price of coal': two hundred and five widows, five hundred and forty-two father-less children and sixty-two dependent parents.

The rescue operation took many weeks. William John, a member of one of the rescue teams, died in a roof fall whilst trying to bring men out of the pit. A month after the explosion two hundred and eighty bodies still had not been recovered. This was the worst coal mining disaster Britain had ever seen and the verdict of accidental death at the Inquest seemed incomprehensible to the victims' families.

◤ Little Mother, Senghenydd, 1913.

◀ Following the explosion canaries were used to check for gas. Many of the deaths were caused by the carbon monoxide which suffocated miners.

▶ Girls Waiting for News, Senghenydd, 1913.

▼◀ Tylorstown Collieries Rescue Squad, 1914.

▼▶ 439 coffins.

66

Soup kitchens and strife

Prolonged periods of industrial conflict marked the early twentieth century. In the Great Unrest between 1908 and 1914 thousands of coal miners, seamen and railway men went on strike. Miners were often locked out of the pits they worked in by the coal owners. In 1910 – 1911 twelve thousand men from the Cambrian Colliery in the Rhondda were involved in a dispute over pay for working in dangerous coal seams. There were riots in Tonypandy as some strikers tried to prevent others from going to work. One miner died, shops were destroyed (but not that of chemist Willie Llewelyn who was a great rugby player), strikers fought the police and eventually troops were sent in by Home Secretary Winston Churchill to keep order. The strikers held out for nearly a year, until starving and penniless, they were forced to return to work on the owners' terms and conditions in October 1911. But their efforts lead to the establishment of the Minimum Wage Act (Mines) in 1912.

Worse was to come as people struggled to survive the depression of the 1920s with no income and no food. Reports of babies being abandoned so distressed Beatrice Green that she worked with Marie Stopes to set up the first hospital-based birth control clinic in Britain in Abertillery in 1925. A women's activist and member of the Abertillery hospital committee, Beatrice was a very determined lady. But a local Baptist minister, Ivor Evans, stirred up a huge public furore, causing such an outcry that the clinic shut down little more than a year later. Beatrice would probably have become the area's MP, but returned from a trip to Russia with an infection which killed her in 1927, leaving a young family motherless.

▲ 500 rabbits to feed the children during the 1910 coal strike, Aberdare.

▼ Aberdare women and girls taking coal from the tips during the 1910 strike.

industry boomed after the British Navy chose Welsh steam coal to power its fleet, by 1913 a quarter of a million men had come to work in the south Wales coalfield. For a time they were among the highest paid workers in the UK. Shops, cafes, pubs and beer houses opened as people recognised the opportunity to make a living serving these new mining communities. Beer houses were also a popular way to supplement family income. The 1830 Beer Act had permitted the front room of a house to be licensed to sell alcohol, and drinking houses became part of the social fabric of many towns.

One of the most successful breweries, the Rhymney Brewery opened in 1839 and less than twenty years later had become the largest in south Wales, mainly due to the efforts of Andrew Buchan the Brewery Manager. The Puddlers Arms in Rhymney was just one of the tied houses associated with the brewery, and many others like the Refiner's Arms, took the name of their clientele. By the 1870s the Rhymney Brewery was delivering 12,500 barrels a year to nearly 30 tied houses.

Italian migrants set up what became known as 'Bracchi' cafes and shops, small family businesses which sent money back home to Italy. There were at least three hundred in Wales by the 1930s. The first Italian shop was established by the Bracchi Brothers in Tonypandy, and led to all future Italian shops and cafes being called 'Bracchi's'. The poet Idris Davies described them as, 'the little Italian shop – where they sell glassy coloured pop'.

73

A group of miners reading newspapers in the Gilfach Goch Workmen's Institute, 1950. The impact of Miners' Institutes and Miners' Libraries on communities was enormous, enriching cultural life and supporting the educational aspirations of many.

Bible, books and Barry Island

As living standards rose and prosperity increased Valley towns became vibrant, busy places with an amazing range of activities specifically for ordinary working people. Miners' and mechanics' institutes, scientific and debating societies became increasingly popular as a means to adult self-education. Just about every town and village had a Miners' Hall or Institute, built and paid for by weekly contributions from the wages of miners and ironworkers. Their libraries and reading rooms were especially valuable in an age before public libraries, but they also housed games rooms, class and committee rooms and a large hall for concerts, lectures and film shows.

Leisure time and paid holidays were just some of the benefits of industrialisation which ordinary people began to enjoy. Thousands of workers from the industrial valleys flocked to the coastal towns of Barry and Porthcawl during 'Miners' Fortnight'.

↑ ◄ Chapel and Sunday School outings descended on the coastal towns in droves.

↑ ► Religion was central to people's lives. During the religious revival of 1904 ministers even held prayer meetings at pit bottom. These ministers, holding miners' lanterns, were about to descend at Penrhiw Colliery.

Wage cuts and hungry families caused riots in Merthyr Tydfil in 1816. Rioters took over the ironworks they worked in, whilst the Crawshays took to the hills. Fourteen year old Penry Williams recorded the scene as the militia tried to restore order.

The Other Revolution

Running in parallel with the Industrial Revolution was another revolution in which the people of south Wales fought to secure the freedoms and political rights we take for granted today. The most rapid rise in the UK population occurred in Monmouthshire between 1800 and 1850, and it was here in the 'Black Domain' that the champions of people power emerged – the Scotch Cattle and the Chartists. There was widespread unrest as ordinary men and women realised they were not going to benefit from the Industrial Revolution. They had little control over their lives, were excluded from power and could not vote in elections. The men who owned the ironworks and collieries also ran Government. Dangerous working conditions, poor housing and unpredictable wages exacerbated worker unhappiness.

The Nantyglo Round Towers symbolise the deepening distrust between owners and workers. Two brothers, Crawshay and Joseph Bailey, the nephews of Richard Crawshay, owned the Nantyglo Ironworks. They were successful but ruthless businessmen and particularly hated by their workers. When the Napoleonic wars came to an end there was a deep economic depression across the Valleys and, fearing for their safety, the brothers constructed two fortified towers at Nantyglo in 1816, the last defensive towers to be built in Britain. Four foot thick walls and solid iron doors with musket holes provided a place of refuge for the ironmasters and their families should their workers revolt.

There was intense hatred of the company owned truck shops. Workers were paid in truck tokens (rather than money) which could only be spent at the company's shop. Prices were higher than other shops and workers were constantly kept in debt. The Monmouthshire magistrates were so concerned about worker unrest that they demanded the House of Commons abolish the truck system in 1830. It took the Merthyr Rising of 1831 for the government to act and officially abolish truck shops. Even so the system continued in many places for another thirty years.

Masked miscreants and masters of disguise

The Scotch Cattle were a secret society of men who blackened their faces, put on headdresses of bull's horns and ventured out at night to intimidate strike breakers. Led by a 'bull' and organised into 'herds', the Scotch Cattle would threaten lives and property, although they had an unspoken rule never to touch food so their victim's children would not suffer. Each valley had its own herd of cattle which carried out attacks in neighbouring valleys, so they would not be recognised. In one attack an innocent woman, Joan Thomas, the wife of a blackleg collier was shot dead in Argoed in 1834. The gunman escaped to America and Edward Morgan, who had been injured in the incident, took the blame and was hanged at Monmouth Gaol.

'Wales is very disturbed now: there are frequent attacks of "Scotch Cattle", or, in other words, of masked miscreants, and Mr. Homfray (the owner of Hirwain Ironworks) has had a letter threatening his life', wrote Lady Charlotte Guest, wife of the Dowlais ironmaster, in her diary in June 1834. *'There came a letter this morning, threatening to "Scotch Cattle" Dowlais House on or about July 2nd, unless all the Irish were discharged from the Works.'*

As well as keeping colliers in line the Cattle would also pressurise the men who acted as agents for the largely absentee coal owners, the truck shop keepers, the colliery officials and the foremen or 'butties', who contracted work and collected the pay. This created a system where there was no defined line between management and workers, which the Scotch Cattle sought to exploit. It was different in the iron industry where management had greater control over the workforce. Butties and those promoted 'top of pit' came under pressure to side with men and not masters (a culture which survived until the Miners' Strike of 1984-85). Men in the Valleys still call their workmates and friends 'butties'.

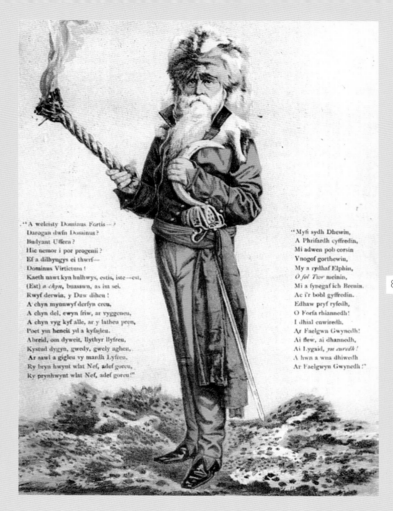

"A weleisty Dominus Fortis—?
Darogan dwfn Dominus?
Budyant Uffern?
Hic nemor i por progenii?
Ef a dilhyngys ei thwrf—
Dominus Virtictua!
Kaeth nawt kyn hulhwys, estis, iste—est,
(Est) a chyn, buasswn, as in sei.
Rwyf derwin, y Duw diheu!
A chyn mynnwyf derfyn creu,
A chyn del, ewyn friw, ar vyggeneu,
A chyn vyg kyf alle, ar y latheu pren,
Poet ym heneti yd a kyfadeu.
Abreid, om dyweit, llythyr llyfreu,
Kystud dygyn, gwedy, gwely agheu,
Ar sawl a gigleu vy mardh Lyfreu,
Ry bryn hwynt wlat Nef, adef goreu,
Ry prynhwynt wlat Nef, adef goreu!"

"Myfi sydh Dhewin,
A Phrifardh cyffredin,
Mi adwen pob corsin
Ynogof gorthewin,
My a rydhaf Elphin,
O fol Twr meinin,
Mi a fynegaf ich Brenin.
Ac i'r bobl cyffredin,
Edhaw pryf ryfedh,
O Forfa rhiannedh!
I dhial enwiredh,
Ar Faelgwn Gwynedh!
Ai flew, ai dhannedh,
Ai Lygaid, yn curedh!
A hwn a wna dhiwedh
Ar Faelgwyn Gwynedh!"

82

▲ One of the more colourful Chartists was Dr William Price, a radical man with an eccentric lifestyle, which included vegetarianism and naturism. Trained as a doctor he set up one of the first worker's medical schemes at the Brown Lennox chain works in Pontypridd. He helped plan the 1839 Chartist march, but fled to Paris, dressed as a woman, when the authorities came looking for him. Towards the end of his life he fought to legalise cremation, cremating his baby son in 1883 for which he was arrested, tried and acquitted, paving the way for his own legal cremation when he died in 1893.

Massacre in Newport

Dear Parents, – I hope this will find you well, as I am myself at present. I shall this night be engaged in a struggle for freedom, and should it please God to spare my life, I shall see you soon; but if not, grieve not for me. I shall fall in a noble cause. My tools are at Mr. Cecil's, and likewise my clothes. These were the words of a young man from Pontypool, George Shell who joined thousands of Chartists as they marched on Newport on the night of November 3rd 1839.

John Frost led two thousand men from Blackwood and Zephaniah Williams led four thousand men down the valley from Blaina, marching over twenty miles in pouring rain to demand the release of local Chartists. A third group of several thousand men, led by William Jones, were strung out along the Malpas Road near Newport waiting for orders. Thomas Protheroe's home at Malpas Court was reported to have been on the Chartist's hit list, where his family would have been kidnapped had they not fled before the marchers arrived.

The authorities in Newport heard rumours that the Chartists were armed and planned to seize the town. They also began to worry that if the Chartists were successful in Newport, they might encourage a national rebellion. As the Chartists approached the Westgate Hotel the soldiers opened fire killing as many as twenty-two men. George Shell was one of those shot by the soldiers in the Westgate Hotel and he was found with his letter pinned to his shirt.

Ten of the victims were buried in unmarked graves at nearby St Woolos Cathedral. Many men were wounded and extracts from the Newport Workhouse register show Chartists admitted with gunshot wounds in the days following the riot. Frost hid in a coal dram after the riot, before returning to the home of his friend John Partridge, where he was arrested, found to be carrying three pistols and charged with high treason. Zephaniah Williams managed to escape to Cardiff and board a ship, only to be captured before the ship sailed.

Events in Newport were watched with concerned interest across south Wales. The Merthyr ironmasters were concerned that there might be Chartist action in Merthyr too. On November 4th 1839 Lady Charlotte Guest wrote in her diary,

There is a report that the Ringleader and ex-magistrate Frost was concerned in the Newport Riot and has been, with many others, arrested; it is also said that some of the poor men, who died of their wounds, showered execrations upon Frost with their latest breath as the instigator of their crime and the cause of their destruction . . . In the midst of the confusion and the anxiety of the present time there is much at which I cannot help being amused. Last night there were several times from fifty to a hundred special constables all in the house, and the succession of suppers and tea-drinkings that went on amongst all that entered was really a curious thing.

High treason

The Chartists' Trial caused immense national interest because everyone knew what the gory penalty for High Treason was. The Shire Hall in Monmouth became the scene of one of the most significant trials in British history. The press descended on the town, filling the pubs and hotels, as did the Home Secretary and the senior judges who were sent to oversee the Trial.

In the preceding months pubs had became important Chartist meeting places and many landlords were Chartist supporters. Some however, were spies for the authorities. The landlord of one of the Monmouth pubs, the Masons Arms in Monnow Street, was threatened and told not to sell beer to men who called themselves Chartists.

A fair trial?

There were two parts to the Special Commission which was set up following events in Newport. A Grand Jury was to decide who should be charged with High Treason, and then the Trials of all the accused would follow. The Grand Jury which began in Monmouth on 10th December 1839, was made up of twenty-three wealthy property owners who were opposed to reform, including some of the most powerful men in Wales, such as the ironmaster Samuel Homfray. He financed a police force in Tredegar, as well as undercover informers who infiltrated local Chartist groups. Another Grand Juror, J.E.W Rolls, doodled on his court papers, drawing three defendants hanging alongside the words 'special fun'! Chartist fears that the Grand Jurors were biased were probably justified.

The Trials opened in Monmouth on 31st December 1839 and a different jury was sworn in to hear prosecution and defence evidence and to decide whether the prisoners were guilty or not. Arguments at the trial of John Frost revolved around whether the Newport attack signaled a national uprising – or whether it was just a local protest. The prosecution emphasised the secrecy surrounding the march and the bullying tactics used against reluctant marchers. There were reports that in the Sirhowy Valley Chartists had gathered outside Carmel Chapel demanding the congregation follow them to Newport. When they refused the Chartists broke into a nearby pub, killed the landlord's dog and demanded beer! The prosecution also claimed there was a plot to stop the mail – which would signal a nationwide uprising.

Chartism was hardly mentioned during the Trial and John Frost had to correct his own counsel who thought that one of the Chartists' demands was to redistribute property.

◀ The Courtroom Scene at the Shire Hall, Monmouth during the trial of the Chartists.

Hanged, drawn and quartered

..... John Frost and you, Zephaniah Williams and you, William Jones.....be drawn on a hurdle to the place of execution and that each of you be hanged by the neck until you be dead and that afterwards the head of each of you be severed from the body and the body of each to be divided into four quarters shall be disposed of as Her Majesty shall think fit.

This grizly sentence was delivered on Thursday 16th January 1840 by Lord Justice Tindal at the end of the Trial. It had taken only half an hour for the jury to find Frost guilty.

After a public outcry at the severity of the death sentences, the Government agreed that the men should be transported for life. On 3rd February 1840 the Chartist leaders were put on board a steamer at Chepstow, the first stage in their five month journey to Australia. John Frost worked for three years as a clerk in Tasmania and eight years as a school teacher, before being pardoned. He returned to the UK in 1856 and by his death in 1877 two of the Charter points had been achieved. William Gould, a former Chartist from Merthyr Tydfil, had patented one of the first secret ballot boxes (although his version wasn't fool proof) and the requirement for MPs to own property had been abolished.

A legacy to be proud of

Despite the severity of punishment, Chartism did not end in 1839. It continued as a major force pushing for political reform. All the Chartists' demands except annual elections are now an integral part of our political system and we take for granted the political freedoms and rights the Newport Chartists died for. Chartism was the world's first independent working-class political movement - and the greatest show of popular protest in Britain's history. It was truly a revolution in people power!

Frost in the condemned cell. Of the fourteen men charged with treason two were found guilty in their absence, three were sentenced to death, five were punished by imprisonment and four were released. The three Chartist leaders sentenced to death – Frost, Jones and Williams – were taken to the condemned cell at Monmouth Gaol, from where Frost could hear scaffolding being constructed ready for his execution.

PEOPLE POWER

REFERENCES AND FURTHER READING

Blaenau Gwent County Borough Council, Aneurin Bevan Heritage Trail

Broomfield, Stuart and Jones, Eurwyn Madoc, Turning Points in Welsh History 1485 – 1914, University of Wales Press, 2004

Culturenet Cymru, 100 Welsh Heroes, Culturenet Cymru, 2004

Davies, John, A History of Wales, Penguin, 2007

Edwards, Susan, Hughesovka, Glamorgan Record Office, 1992

Hayman, Richard, Working Iron in Merthyr Tydfil, Merthyr Tydfil Heritage Trust, 1989

Jones, Bill & Thomas Beth, Coal's Domain, National Museum Wales, 1993

Jones, David J V, The Last Rising – The Newport Chartist Insurrection of 1839, 1985

Lewis-Jones, Keith, Noteworthy Merthyr Citizens, Merthyr Tydfil Heritage Trust, 2008

Lord, Peter, The Francis Crawshay Worker Portraits, University of Wales Centre for Advanced Welsh and Celtic Studies, 1996

Lord, Peter, The Visual Culture of Wales: Industrial Society, University of Wales Press, Cardiff, 1998

Needham, Dennis, Welsh Canals – then and now, Y Lolfa, 1998

Nichols, Reginald, Pontypool and Usk Japanware, 1981

Owen, John A., A short history of the Dowlais Ironworks, Merthyr Tydfil Library Service, 2001

Porch, Richard, A Short History of the Hafod Copperworks, City and County of Swansea

Porch, Richard, Swansea, History you can see, Tempus Publishing, 2005

Richards, Alun John, Tinplate in Wales, Llygad Gwalch, 2008

Rowson, Stephen and Wright, Ian L., The Glamorganshire and Aberdare Canals, Black Dwarf Publications, 2001

Rothwell, Thomas, Views of Swansea in the 1790's, Glamorgan Archives, 1991

Tawe River Navigation Heritage Trail

Torfaen County Borough Council, Cadw, RCAHMW, Nomination of the Blaenavon Industrial Landscape for Inclusion on the World Heritage List

Thomas, Tydfil, Poor Relief in Merthyr Tydfil Union in Victorian Times, Glamorgan Archive Service Publication, 1992

Trett, Bob, Newport Transporter Bridge, Newport Museum & Art Gallery,

Wakelin, Peter, Blaenavon Ironworks and World Heritage Landscape, Cadw, 2006

Williams, David, John Frost – A Study in Chartism, 1939

Whittle, Elizabeth, The Historic Gardens of Wales, Cadw, 1992

Williams, Gwyn A., When Was Wales? Penguin, 1991

Williams, Matthew, The Essential Cardiff Castle, Scala Publishers, 2008